NINJA

Volume IV: Legacy of the Night Warrior

**Text and verses
by Stephen K. Hayes**

Editor: Mike Lee
Graphic Design: Karen Massad

Art Production:
Junko Sadjadpour,
Amy Goldman Koss

©Ohara Publications, Inc.
All rights reserved
Printed in the United States of America
Library of Congress Card Number: 84-61831
ISBN: 0-89750-102-0

Second Printing 1985

 OHARA PUBLICATIONS, INC.
BURBANK • CALIFORNIA

DEDICATION

This book is dedicated with love to
Christine and Jane,
fellow seedlings on the forest floor of life
growing tall together
in the sunshine of our days.

ABOUT THE AUTHOR

Now recognized as the Western world's foremost authority on the art and practice of the legendary Japanese art of ninjutsu, author Stephen K. Hayes began his quest for warrior enlightenment as a teenager in southwestern Ohio. His years of personal sacrifice and determined searching throughout his young adulthood have subsequently earned him a unique role in the world martial arts community. As the one Westerner responsible for introducing the authentic teachings of the shinobi night warriors to the English speaking world, Stephen K. Hayes is a living bridge between the timeless wisdom of the East and the fresh vigor of the West, between the past and the future.

As the first American ever to be accepted as a direct disciple of ninjutsu grandmaster Masaaki Hatsumi of Noda City, Japan, Stephen K. Hayes was exposed to an art that was, until the early 1970s, totally unknown to all but a handful of practitioners who had managed to gain entrance to the grandmaster's dojo. In September of 1978, Stephen K. Hayes became the first non-Japanese person in the history of the art of ninjutsu ever to be awarded the title of *Shidoshi*, (teacher of the warrior ways of enlightenment).

Subsequently, the author was granted the permission to establish his own family branch of Dr. Hatsumi's Bujinkan dojo system in the Western world. Teaching a universally oriented adaptation of the art that generations of Japanese warriors have sheltered from extinction over the centuries, Stephen K. Hayes' worldwide network of training halls provides students all over the globe with the opportunity to become a direct and active part of living nin-po tradition and history.

ACKNOWLEDGEMENT

✳

As a black belt instructor of the martial arts, with my own school and a large group of students, I had spent years in pursuit of the ultimate system of warrior knowledge. I had an idea of what that knowledge might look like when I finally found it, and how it might be manifested through my own life once I had embodied it. My anticipations could not have been further from the eventual truth I was to experience as a student of the grandmaster of ninjutsu.

The ninja warrior's abilities far exceed the limits of crude bone and muscle speed and strength that I had worked so diligently to cultivate before meeting the teacher who would eventually be the guidepost pointing towards the invincibility I sought. In the end, it took me years of "unlearning" just to be able to approach the basics of the awesome skills that my teacher could casually embody in his own effortless flow of powers.

This book is then an acknowledgement of the warrior teacher, Dr. Masaaki Hatsumi. In apology to the grandmaster, it must be noted that this volume can only hint at the ultimate application of the warrior's influence on his own universe. However, perhaps even that small reflection of Dr. Hatsumi's art will serve as an inspiration towards continued growth for those in the world seeking martial truth.

CONTENTS

CHAPTER ONE
THE UNFOLDING STORY: In ancient times, he
is a military advisor, a bringer of good fortune   11

CHAPTER TWO
THE FIVE ELEMENTS OF ESCAPE: His close
communion with nature gives him the wisdom
to survive   23

CHAPTER THREE
FLOWING ACTION: Living in the flow of action, his success is the most natural outcome
of combat   47

CHAPTER FOUR
KUNOICHI, THE DEADLY FLOWER: She fights
alongside her brother ninja, defeating even
those of greater strength   107

CHAPTER FIVE
THE FORCE OF INTENTION: Using esoteric
sensitivity training, he learns to feel the intentions of others   149

AFTERWORD
AN INTERVIEW WITH STEPHEN HAYES: The
author speaks on the state of his ninjutsu art
in Western society   181

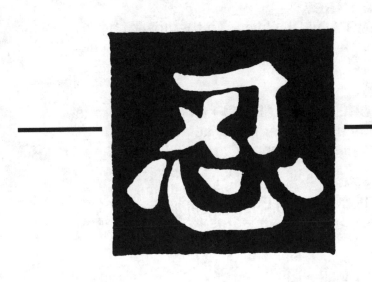

CHAPTER 1

THE UNFOLDING STORY

Yours is a legacy of service to those in need,
protection to those in distress
and strength to those who are overpowered.
Your guide is nin-po
silent means of working your will without actions.
Your reward is spiritual growth
and an active role in the scheme of totality.

The historical art of Japan's invisible ninja warriors of the night has its roots woven deep in the ancient past of the enigmatic island nation of the Rising Sun. Unlike the more conventional and easily accessible sport and recreation martial arts that are so popular in our modern society, it is almost impossible to determine an exact time or place or founder associated with the birth of ninjutsu. Korean tae kwon do can be traced back to its founding in the 1950s. Japanese judo can be traced back to its origins in the late 1800s. Even the majority of the traditional sword arts and sports of Japan have documented founders and births traceable to the 1500s.

ANCIENT HISTORY

The art of ninjutsu, however, reaches back over a millenium to an age in Japan's antiquity that predates even the history of the famous elite samurai warrior caste. The basic body of knowledge that later came to be called ninjutsu, or *nin-po* in its higher order, was at first regarded as merely an unconventional way of handling life situations and accomplishing the necessary. What eventually went on to become a highly systematic and scientific method of combat, espionage, and danger prevention, began as a shadowy counterculture, a forced reaction against the mainstream of Japanese political, military, economic, and social traditions.

Forerunners of the Ninja

The art seems to have developed from an entwining of religious and military backgrounds to produce a uniquely Japanese approach toward using nature, cosmic laws, human psychology and physiology, and the inevitable cycles of history as a means of ensuring physical and spiritual survival. The forerunners of the ninja included *sennin* and *gyoja* (warrior hermits), *yamabushi* and *shugenja* (mountain mystics), refugee Chinese taoist sages and military officers, as well as unfortunate Japanese *bushi* who found themselves homeless and masterless after their forces had been routed by others.

The First Ninja

The original people who were later referred to as ninja filled adivsory roles in the camps of military rulers vying for control over the various regions of Japan. The true ninja was a "bringer of good fortune" to those who had the power and influence to assist the ninja's families in finding peaceful and stable lives. Because of the original ninja's closeness with nature and inclinations toward what others described as "occult" powers, they could provide valuable perspectives and counsel to those who were more familiar with conventional politics and warfare. The ninja had trusted contacts or direct subordinates who could move into areas closed to conventional forces for reconnaissance, and also possessed an insightful mind that could see into the future to evaluate any currently formulating plans.

In most cases, ninjutsu *ryu* (traditions or systems) came to be formed as one generation after another carried on the stealthful methods of survival handed down from the elders of the family to the younger members. The ryu would not be "founded" as such, but rather, would evolve itself up from seemingly unrelated fragments of history in the making. The Togakure ryu of ninjutsu, for example, was well into its third generation before its members began to refer to their body of developing knowledge and tradition as a documented ryu based on the experiences and teachings of their ancestor Daisuke Togakure in the late 1100s. The Gyokko ryu ninja system of *koshijutsu* (unarmed combat), the oldest of all the ryu that now make up the training curriculum of the Bujinkan Dojo of grandmaster Masaaki Hatsumi, evolved for many generations in the Iga region of Japan before the members of that particular martial tradition decided to name their method after the Chinese refugee warrior Cho Gyokko, who had first introduced his revolutionary concepts of unarmed fighting to the rural Japanese locals aiding him in his new country of political exile.

Formation of Ryu

Other ninjutsu ryu came into existence as the tides of Japanese economics and politics became more turbulent from the 1300s onward. Ryu were often formed as families found themselves outside the mainstream of military and political developments, where creative thinking and action were the last remaining possiblities for guaranteeing survival. Other ryu were only temporarily established for the purpose of aiding the cause of a specific regional lord, military group, or religious order and then later disbanded when no longer needed. Some ninjutsu ryu were regional in nature, and came together as a result of geographical politics. Still other ryu were based around extensive bodies of knowledge, experience, and wisdom collected by one specific individual.

The documented historical ninja ryu of Japan varied in size and importance from small collections of a few family members to vast regional networks involving hundreds of people who often did not even know each other and were connected only through their common loyalties to a single overseer. The following names are a partial listing of a few of the more influential or historically significant ninjutsu ryu and their founders, regions of operation, or military and political affiliations:

- *Nakagawa ryu* ninjutsu was based in Aomori Prefecture, organized by Nakagawa Kohayato.
- *Haguro ryu* ninjutsu was based in Yamagata Prefecture, and was said to have been developed by the warrior ascetics of Haguro Mountain.
- *Uesugi ryu* ninjutsu was established for Uesugi Kenshin as a military espionage organization by Usami Suruganokami Sadayuki in Niigata Prefecture.
- *Kaji ryu* ninjutsu was founded by Kaji Ominokami Kagehide, a student of the founder of Uesugi ryu, but was also linked to the roots of Iga's *Hattori ryu* ninjutsu.
- *Matsumoto ryu* ninjutsu was based in Tochigi Prefecture.
- *Matsuda ryu* ninjutsu was based in Ibaraki Prefecture.

- *Koyo ryu*, *Ninko ryu*, and *Takeda ryu* ninjutsu, founded by Takeda Shingen for intelligence gathering, used wandering monks and merchants as agents.
- *Fuma* nin-po, based in Kanagawa Prefecture, established by Fuma Kotaro, specialized in guerrilla warfare.
- *Akiba ryu*, *Ichizen ryu*, based in Aichi Prefecture, were established by Hachisuka Koroku Masakatsu who was a famous ninja from this area.
- *Mino ryu* ninjutsu, based in Gifu Prefecture, was developed during the rule of Saito Dosan, and included the Kurokawa ninja group of Koga.
- *Echizen ryu* ninjutsu was established in Toyama Prefecture by Iga ninja fleeing the attack of Oda Nobunaga.
- *Yoshitsune ryu* ninjutsu, based in Fukui Prefecture, was developed for Yoshitsune Minamoto as a blend of espionage methods taught by Ise Saburo and yamabushi teachings.
- *Koga ryu* ninjutsu was a regional tradition made up of over fifty families.
- *Iga ryu* ninjutsu was a regional tradition made up of several key families, most notably the Hattori and Momochi clans.
- *Negoro ryu*, founded by Suginobo Myosan, firearms master; *Saiga ryu*, firearms and explosives specialists; *Natori ryu*, founded by Natori Sanjuro Masatake, author of *Sho Nin Ki* ninjutsu reference work; and *Kishu ryu* ninjutsu—were all based in Wakayama Prefecture.
- *Bizen ryu* ninjutsu was based in Okayama Prefecture.
- *Fukushima ryu* ninjutsu, transmitted by Nojirijiro Jirouemon Narimasa was based in Shimane Prefecture.
- *Kuroda ryu* ninjutsu was based in Fukuoka Prefecture, in support of Kuroda family government.
- *Nanban ryu* ninjutsu was based in Nagasaki Prefecture.
- *Satsuma* nin-po was based in Kagoshima Prefecture in support of Shimazu family government.

The vast majority of ninjutsu ryu*, all save a small handful, died out long before the Meiji Restoration in 1868. Once unification and enforced peace came to Japan in the 1600s, the need for extensive intelligence

---

Author's footnote:

The foregoing list of ninjutsu ryu names are a part of the past history of Japan, just as the names Sitting Bull and "Swampfox" Marion are parts of American history. Anyone claiming to be teaching the methods of any of these ryu will of course have to have extensive documentation to prove that the scrolls donated to the museums are actually frauds, and that he has indeed inherited the authority of the ryu which Japanese historians and scholars have verified as dead. Students beware! Would you really want to model your life after that of a person who would lie to you about his credentials in order to coerce your respect or get some of your money?

gathering networks and thorough training in the brutal arts of life or death all but vanished. As the need for the skills of ninjutsu dwindled, so did the numbers of practitioners who devoted their energies to living the shinobi arts. Just as there is no French underground resistance movement now that there are no longer German occupation troops holding French territory, the urgency of the original ninja families also faded with time and with the establishment of new Japanese governmental policies.

Today, the only authentic historical ninjutsu ryu still surviving in Japan have been inherited by grandmaster Masaaki Hatsumi of Noda City, Japan. The remains of the other ryu can be seen on public display in museums and galleries throughout Japan. Scrolls of grandmaster authority, weapons, and even battle garb, in some rare cases, can be found as silent testimony to their system's demise.

Once a ryu died out, the last remaining grandmaster was expected to destroy the tradition's scrolls and manuscripts to prevent the ryu's name and reputation from being dragged into disrepute. In some cases, the material was left behind, or sold off by heirs who did not understand the significance of the contents.

MODERN HISTORY

In the middle of the 19th century, the island nation of Japan opened up to foreign trade and influence. The once-powerful Tokugawa family, who had ruled Japan as military dictators for over 200 years, relinquished their control over the government, and the duties of ruling the country were returned to the imperial family. The elite samurai class that had provided law, order, and stability to Japanese life for almost 700 years was abolished, and Japan raced to adopt the newly discovered western modes of culture.

During the Meiji Era that followed the opening of Japan in 1868, two important government slogans changed the face of life in Japan. The *Fukoku kyohei* stated the new government's aim was to "Enrich the nation and strengthen the military." The second slogan of *Bunmei kaika* provided the means of building up the country by "opening up the culture" to the influence of foreign ways. The old traditions like the warrior skills of individual combat came to be seen as *yaban* (barbaric) and the military leaders of Japan turned to Europe for guidance in modern military tactics.

As one result of this cultural upheaval, the martial arts were stripped of their martial significance and transformed into sports and personal development exercise systems. Battlefield methods of life-protecting combat were fractionalized into pieces of ritual movement with one specific weapon, or games of skills with a limited set of body movements. Comprehensive warrior training covering a broad scope of applications was seen as a relic from the dead past, something useless in the modern age.

Those martial artists who pioneered the change from warfare to self-improvement are now legendary. Judo's Kano, aikido's Uyeshiba, and karate's Funakoshi captured the hearts of their nation with their new, safer, limited, and sanitized versions of what had once been rough-and-tumble combat methods in which injury was quite often a part of the training. The new martial systems were heralded as "gentlemanly" adaptations of the old and obsolete warrior methods.

Not all master teachers of the martial arts embraced this change in approach, however. Many of the old warriors cautioned against the rush to abandon what had been their legacy for generations. For the large part, however, their pleas fell on deaf ears and they gradually faded into obscurity with progress into the 20th century.

Ishitani Trains Takamatsu

Such was the case of Takakage Matsutaro Ishitani, whose ancestors had been high-ranking *chunin* ninja in the troops of Iga ryu ninjutsu *jonin* Hanzo Hattori three centuries earlier. As the 26th grandmaster of the *Kuki Shinden ryu happo hiken* (secret weapon arts) of ninjutsu, a system originally founded by Izumo Kanja Yoshiteru, Ishitani refused to dilute his method to appeal to the masses now more interested in sporting competition or zen movement.

Obscurity for Ishitani was being relegated to doing security work at the Takamatsu family's match factory in Kobe, the closest thing he could find for application of the clandestine specialities he had inherited from an older and less secure age. Without students or a dojo, the grandmaster of Kuki Shinden ryu resigned himself to living out the rest of his life as an anachronism from another time. He was prepared, like other ninja masters before him, to destroy all his secret scrolls and weapons before his death so that no unqualified impostors would later defame the name of his ryu by posing as a master teacher of the Kuki Shinden ryu. If there were no worthy heir, the legacy would be taken to the grave with him.

Through his work at the Takamatsu match factory, Ishitani came to meet the young son of the factory's owner. A special relationship soon developed, and Takakage Matsutaro Ishitani knew that he had found the heir he had been seeking in the young Toshitsugu Takamatsu. Already an experienced practitioner of *Koto ryu koppojutsu* and *Shinden Fudo ryu dakentaijutsu*, as taught to him by his grandfather Shinryuken Masamitsu Toda, the young Takamatsu leaped at the chance to learn the specialities of the Kuki Shinden ryu from his new mentor Ishitani. In an age that had outgrown the true warrior ways, it was a perfect matching of student and teacher.

Book covers of antique ninja books, courtesy of the Iga Ryu Ninja Yashiki Museum in Ueno-Shi, Japan.

Ishitani first taught Toshitsugu Takamatsu the eight-part *happo* method that included:

1. *Taijutsu* (unarmed combat), *hichojutsu* (leaping), *nawanage* (rope throwing).
2. *Koppojutsu* (bone smashing technique), *jutaijutsu* (grappling).
3. *Yarijutsu* (spear technique), *naginatajutsu* (halberd skills).
4. *Bojutsu* (long staff fighting), *jojutsu* (cane technique), *hanbojutsu* (stick fighting).
5. *Senban nage* (shuriken star throwing), *tokenjutsu* (blade throwing).
6. *Kajutsu* (fire and explosives), *suijutsu* (water techniques).
7. *Chiku jo gunryaku heiho* (military tactics and fortress design and penetration).
8. *Onshinjutsu* (art of invisibility), *hensojutsu* (disguise).

Next, the young disciple was taught the *hiken* (secret sword) method, which included the Kuki Shinden ryu approach to handling *ken* (swords), *kodachi* (short blades), and *jutte* (anti-sword truncheons).

Toshitsugu Takamatsu trained hard and assimilated the teachings, and was eventually granted the scrolls, weapons, and title of 27th grandmaster of the Kuki Shinden tradition. Ishitani had found his heir.

As a child, Toshitsugu Takamatsu had been shuttled through a succession of nine foster mothers. His childhood had not been a happy one, and security was but a fleeting concept in his young life. Takamatsu had grown up tough and determined, as evidenced by a Kobe newspaper report of the 14-year-old having soundly thrashed a gang of older attackers in an alleyway. The young Takamatsu therefore came to rely on his grandparents as the single point of stability in his life.

Shinryuken Masamitsu Toda, Toshitsugu Takamatsu's grandfather, had been supervisor of sword teachers for the Tokugawa shogun's government school in their home region. Much less well-known was the fact that Toda was the 32nd in the line of grandmasters of the Togakure ryu ninjutsu tradition. Following his instruction of the Koto ryu and Shinden Fudo ryu methods, the grandmaster began to train his grandson in the esoteric art of the Togakure ninja warriors; climbing, stalking, and evasion techniques were introduced along with the weapon and unarmed skills that the young Takamatsu had been practicing since late childhood.

Ineligible for military service because of a ruptured eardrum which he carried as a souvenir of fight during his teen years, Takamatsu took off on his own when he was 21. A career at the match factory paled in comparison with the thought of the adventure that waited across the sea in China, then considered to be the land of fortune in Japan's future. Journeying from north to south through the vast country. Takamatsu found numerous opportunities to rely on his warrior skills for the protection of his life.

After the rough and tumble years in China and a period of living in the wilderness of the mountains in Japan, Takamatsu returned to his home in 1919 to study and be ordained as a *mikkyo* (secret doctrine) priest of the Tendai-shu on Kyoto's Mt. Hihei. By age 30, Toshitsugu Takamatsu had straddled the two realms of warrior invincibility and spiritual power as a recognized master of both.

Takamatsu Trains Hatsumi

Masaaki Hatsumi began his martial arts training at the age of seven, when he began practicing with his father's *bokuto* (wooden sword). From that point he went on to train in all of the popular Japanese martial arts of the wartime era, eventually earning teaching ranks in karate, aikido, and judo. The martial arts and theater arts were the passions of his life in his teen and young adult years.

During the postwar years in Japan, however, the young Hatsumi was shocked to see how quickly and skillfully the American occupation soldiers he taught picked up the technique of judo. The huge Americans used their size and natural athletic inclinations to learn in months what it took the Japanese years of training to obtain. What was the use of training in a system if others could surpass your efforts by mere size alone? There had to be some sort of ultimate warrior system for all situations, thought the young martial arts teacher.

Through his *kobudo* (ancient weapons) teacher, Masaaki Hatsumi learned of a teacher named Toshitsugu Takamatsu, of Kashiwabara City to the west of the Iga region in Japan. As a last hope at finding someone who could teach a living warrior art and not a recreational sport or system of rigid lifeless kata, the young Hatsumi traveled across Honshu island to seek out the teacher he had been seeking for a lifetime.

The veteran battler Takamatsu was well into his 60s when he met the young man who would eventually become his spiritual heir and the next grandmaster of ninjutsu. For Takamatsu, that first meeting was more of a reunion than an introduction. In a poem to Masaaki Hatsumi, Takamatsu wrote:

Long ago, I was an accomplished warrior
of the koppojutsu tradition.
I was courageous and as intense as the flame,
even in battle against violent animals.
I have a heart that is like the wildflowers of the meadows,
and yet straight and true as the bamboo.
Not even ten thousand enemies can cause me fear.
Who is there in the world who would keep alive
this will of the warrior's heart?
There you are, this one sent to me by the warrior gods.
I have been waiting for you
through all the ages.

For years, Masaaki Hatsumi suffered his rough apprenticeship under the direction of the ninja grandmaster with the heart like wildflowers and hands like a tiger's. Eventually, Dr. Hatsumi went on to inherit the title of grandmaster of the nine warrior traditions carried by his teacher Toshitsugu Takamatsu.

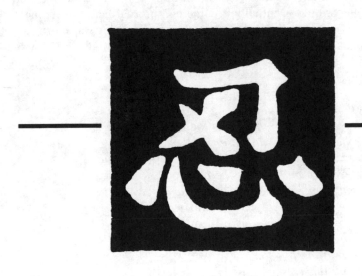

CHAPTER 2

THE FIVE ELEMENTS OF ESCAPE

In the lessons of nature
  there is wisdom for the ninja.
The mystical combatant becomes
  the whisper of the leaves
  the smell of the earth
  the taste of the sea
  in order to accomplish what must be done
  and live to celebrate
  yet another day.

T he legendary Japanese warrior art of ninjutsu developed in mountain and marsh wilderness territories far remote from the feudal emperor's capital in Kyoto. Because the historical ninja had to face overwhelming odds, with the enemy often being government troops who were far better equipped, stronger in numbers, and official representatives of the legal establishment controlling the region, physical survival often entailed a working familiarity with the forces of nature and the cycles of the seasons as a means of increasing the likelihood of success for these outlawed economic and religious rebels who developed the shinobi arts.

As a means of passing on skills to younger family members and preserving the knowledge in a manner that would allow seasoned operatives to recall vital instructions even in moments of extreme life-threatening stress, the ninja of south central Japan developed a series of working models from nature. The models were used as codes to simplify the process of understanding and remembering. They were not employed in attempting the impossible task of classifying all potential methods with all their physical details.

In the nature lore of ninjutsu, there developed two distinct systems that today are commonly referred to as "five element" theories.

Go-Dai

Of great importance in understanding the ninja combat method, one theory, the ninja's *go-dai* (five major elemental manifestations), derived from the nin-po mikkyo Himalayan tantric spiritual teachings, includes the following codes:

Chi—earth (solid matter)
Sui—water (liquids)
Ka—fire (energy transformation)
Fu—wind (gasses)
Ku—primordial ether (subatomic source of all elements)

Go-Gyo

Another "five element" theory, the *go-gyo* (five element transformations), stemmed from Chinese taoist teachings that found their way into feudal Japan by way of authorized cultural exchanges, as well as covert instruction provided by refugee Chinese generals and priests seeking sanctuary in Japan following the destruction that accompanied the collapse of China's Tang Dynasty in the Tenth Century. Unlike the go-dai system that cataloged the elements during the ever-continuing formation of the universe, the go-gyo system stems from the *in* and *yo* (*yin* and *yang* in Chinese) polarity theory and catalogs the cycle of transformation that continuously takes place in the realm of material objects. The five elemental transformations include the following contraction and expansion codes:

Sui—water (dissolving)
Moku—wood (growing)
Ka—fire (evaporating)
Do—earth (solidifying)
Kin—metal (hardening)

It should be emphasized that these five elemental codes were developed as symbols typifying the stages through which all matter passes. They are not meant to be taken as literal classifications of trees, rocks, water, and so forth. All phenomena continue to pass through these transformations in a cyclical pattern, for which the five codes were assigned as a means of better understanding. The five do not exist as five separate entities in themselves, but rather reflect the quality of blending or emerging from one state into another. The cycle has no real beginning or end, either. The observer will note that the cycle seems to begin at that stage in the rise and fall of energy wherever he or she happens to first direct attention.

Each stage of the transformation process can be seen to lead naturally into the next in a series of never-ending supporting relationships. Water (sinking condensation) produces wood, wood (up-reaching growth) produces fire, fire (expanding free energy) produces solid earth, earth (compacting) produces metal, and metal (hardening) in turn produces water. This natural five-element code system works equally well whether used for medical healing and strengthening purposes or applied as a means of analyzing the destinies of nations.

Goton-po

Rationally, the symbols can also be followed in a series of destructive or inhibiting relationships by altering the perspective or progress of the flow. Water (melting) can put out fire, fire (rising energy) can soften metal, metal (hardening) can cut down wood, wood (growing) can break up earth, and earth (solidifying) can dam up water. This subduing symbolism is in turn the basis for the historical ninja's *goton-po* (five-element escape method).

Because the ninja families of ancient Japan were part of an underground counterculture that existed at the annoyance of the established samurai bureaucracy power structure, self-protection and the prevention of danger often entailed covert actions by mere individuals opposing the might of major troop formations. These tremendous odds made conventional honorable warfare not only illegal but impossible as well. Therefore, all approaches to survival, from psychological deception to homemade black powder to blending with the elements of nature, had to be considered by the ninja.

At face value, the ninja's goton-po could, of course, serve as a guide for vanishing from the sight of the enemy. The night warrior could imitate or blend in with the rocks and earth, trees, bodies of water, or utilize fire and smoke or metal objects as a means of enhancing his or her chances of successful escape. This is the more obvious application of the

goton-po five-element theory.

Dotonjutsu is the use of the earth element to aid in escape. This application includes a knowledge of the geography of the area of operation, the use of natural terrain features for concealment, and the strategic employment of terrain as a means of hindering and discouraging the enemy's pursuit. Skills of land navigation, efficient walking and running methods, and a working knowledge of how to operate a wide range of vehicles are also parts of ninjutsu's dotonjutsu.

Suitonjutsu is the use of the water element to aid in escape and evasion. This application of the go-gyo theory includes the use of still or moving water as a means of penetrating or leaving enemy territory, the use of water for concealment, and the use of streams, bodies of water, and even induced flooding as a means of detaining or hindering pursuers. Methods of water navigation, stealth swimming and underwater action, and a knowledge of boat and flotation device operation are also parts of the ninja's suitonjutsu.

Katonjutsu is the use of the fire element to assist the ninja in escape actions. This interpretation of the goton-po five-element tactics includes the use of smoke and fire as cover or distraction, as well as a knowledge of the preparation and employment of explosives. Also part of ninjutsu's katonjutsu since the 16th Century is a working ability with all types of firearms that could be used by or against the ninja and his or her family.

Mokutonjutsu is the use of wood and plants as a means of aiding the ninja to evade an enemy. Trees and brush could be used for concealment or undetected viewing posts, or could be employed to hinder large groups of armored or mounted troops attempting pursuit. The use of plants as natural medicine or poisons also constitutes an aspect of ninjutsu's mokutonjutsu, as does a working knowledge of structural configuration and carpentry.

Kintonjutsu is the employment of metal objects to assist in escape and evasion. Metal applications include all tools needed to gain access or escape from locked and barricaded structures, climb or perch on high structures or natural formations, or fight off the attack of an enemy who would restrain the ninja.

Less obvious is the deeper symbolism of the goton-po as a series of lesson blocks dealing with the transformation of energies in a natural manner so as to be able to guide and overcome the enemy's attack, or at least create a false and yet totally believable perception of reality in the enemy's mind. Growing, rising energy (wood) leads to free-moving expansive energy (fire), unless it encounters factors of hardening (metal) which inhibits or stops growth. Melting, newly flowing energy (water) leads to growing, rising energy (wood), unless it is inhibited by solidifying tendencies (earth). In a combat scenario, free-moving expansive energy (fire) that manifests itself as speed and power will eventually run out, which leads to a need to slow down (earth) and scientifically hold ground, unless the reliance on speed is inhibited by energy-conserving tendencies that turn the fighting action into relaxed flowing motions (water).

It is important to emphasize that the ninja's five-element go-gyo theory of using natural cyclical tendencies is based on a series of graphic symbols from nature, and does not represent a system of literal interpretations of the so-called elements. "Metal produces water which produces wood, but is conquered by fire which is in turn conquered by water," is really a coded way of reminding ourselves that hardness eventually softens, and softness produces upward-rising energy, but the tendency toward hardness is inhibited by aspects that would lead to lighter, freer energy, and expansive rising energy is in turn brought down by qualities of melting or flowing. As with all else that is ninjutsu, the go-gyo five elements are a powerful tool that can lead to the understanding that produces enlightenment, if only we can reach behind the surface and grasp the hidden significance.

DOTONJUTSU
(Use of Earth)

**Concealment in
a Rock Formation**
Using a rock and the shadow it casts is a good use of dotonjutsu (earth escape method). (1) Blending in with the desert surroundings, you can avoid detection. (2) The severe contrast of light and shadow also helps to hide you from sight even when you

3

begin to move out if you are wearing dark clothing. Dark shapes are difficult for the eyes to distinguish in a shadow if the surrounding light is stark and intense. (3&4) In this way, you can remain hidden until it is safe to leave your hiding place entirely.

4

1

2

Concealment from a Guard

(1-4) In this example of *dotonjutsu* (use of earth as a means of concealment) you become a part of something familiar to the bored guard, such as a rock grouping. He has walked this route many times before without inci-

3

dent, and his attention is not attracted to benign landscape features he is accustomed to taking for granted. Such "boring" objects make excellent cover in which to conceal yourself.

4

Concealment in Low Vegetation

Using dotonjutsu (earth escape method), (1-4) you can use a washed out area on a slope as a place to remain out of sight, staying close to the ground and allowing the low vegetation to conceal you in the same way it conceals the ground, until

the proper time comes to move. Blending in and becoming part of the environment so as to remain undetected is also a matter of considering the nature of the particular element you have chosen to use as your method.

Climbing a Rock Face

To scale a rock face, the body (1) is flattened out and allowed to relax into the surface of the rock. The limbs stretch out so that bone as well as muscle carries the load of the shifting weight. (2) You must hold three points secured while you (3-6) move a fourth, either hand or foot, into higher position. That way, your body will have a better chance of holding firmly should the new hand or foot position prove to be unstable. The three-point method also aids in quieter climbing.

Scaling a Wall

(1) To escape capture, or avoid a needless confrontation, the *dotonjutsu* (earth escape) method can be used to run right up a wall in order to evade a pursuer. (2-4) By generating enough speed, the momentum of your body carries

you into the wall, giving you enough force against it to enable you to use your feet to propel your body upwards along the surface of the vertical obstacle, and (5) facilitate your escape.

SUITONJUTSU
(Use of Water)

1

2

Concealment in a Pond

(1&2) To avoid detection, or as a means of escape, water can be used as a hiding place. Again, because one does not normally think of water as a good hiding place, it makes an excellent one. You are able to hide below the surface of a pond by breathing through a thin tube that has the appearance of a reed, becoming yourself a part of the water by being calm, and therefore not creating any movement that would disturb the natural appearance of the water under those particular conditions.

KATONJUTSU
(Use of Smoke and Fire)

Distraction and Intimidation

(A) The use of smoke and fire created terror in an age when all structures were comprised of wood, rice paper, and straw. (B) The use of firearms and explosives was also a crucial aspect of the ninja's fire approach to escape and avoidance.

MOKUTONJUTSU
(Use of Wood)

Climbing a Column

As a means of evading discovery, proper tree and column climbing techniques from the ninja's use of wood for escape are taught to contemporary age students. Note that (1&2) your body is held upright and close to the tree trunk so that the feet can wedge in by using the body's weight, and not muscle tension, to hold the position while (3&4) your hands reach up for a higher hold. Then (5) the feet are brought up to a higher position.

2

4

5

KINTONJUTSU
(Use of Metal)

Tools and Weapons

(A) The *kaginawa* (the ninja's rope and grappling hook) is used as a climbing aid, or for transporting gear and equipment. (B) The Togakure ryu ninja's *shuko* (hand claws) are hooked over objects to be climbed, and never slammed straight into solid surfaces. Contrary to modern belief, the shuko were not tools common to most ancient ninjutsu ryu, but rather were secret inventions of Iga Province Togakure family ninja. (C)

Kaginawa

Shuko

The *shuriken* (throwing blades), perhaps the most famous of the legendary ninja tools, are a prime example of the ninja's creative thinking in applying the principles of the kintonjutsu. (D) *Tetsubishi* (iron spikes) are yet another example of the kintonjutsu principles of using metal to aid escape. These are on display in the Iga-Ueno City Ninja Museum. Thrown in the path of pursuers, the spikes impede the enemy's pursuit.

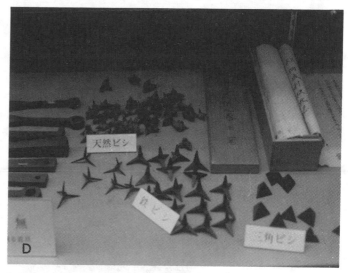

Tetsubishi

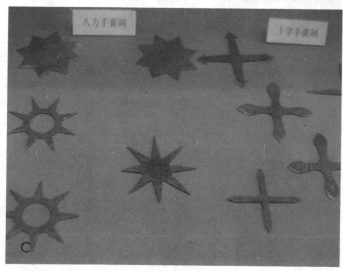

Shuriken

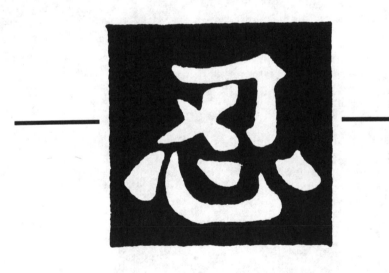

CHAPTER 3

FLOWING ACTION

Swiftness of fist
  power behind the kick—
  the vast collection of techniques.
These are but the first step
  of the journey to warrior invincibility.
Why then are so many content to stop learning
  and put down roots
  at the entrance to the path?

O nce a student of the warrior arts completes his or her training in the fundamentals of physical self-protection combat, it is then time to go on and personalize the art so as to make the fundamentals an integral part of the personality—in effect, "forgotten" as special and separate in and of themselves.

This process can work in two ways. The student can adapt his or her ways of moving so as to conform to the art. The movements are internalized and the body ends up with a new way of moving, as in the *kata* (form) method of training. On the other hand, the student can adapt the art to fit his or her ways of moving. The purpose and details of the techniques are internalized and the body ends up with additional possibilities for ways of moving, as in the *waza* (technique) method of training.

The kata method of dramatically altering the way the student's body moves from the inside can cause frustration because of the rigid manner in which the body's natural movement patterns are ignored or disrupted.

The waza method of quickly altering the way the body moves from the outside by supplying new ways to handle familiar situations can provide frustration through the unstructured manner in which the body's learned movement patterns are expected to adapt freely to the new material.

For balanced growth through training in the warrior arts, one must change from the inside as well as the outside. To restrict training to only one of the two methods is to encourage only half the growth possible. Although for a brief period results do seem to appear more quickly, this is simply because the contrasting half of the training process is not present to cause doubts in the body or mind.

Kotsu

The key to progress in the self-protection methods that characterize the art of ninjutsu is a *kotsu* (essence) approach to training. By combining aspects of training in both movement principles and application concepts, the student can develop a balanced ability that blends skills of effective body dynamics with practical responses to attacks. With that kind of training approach, even from the first few instruction sessions, the student will come away with some useable concrete results that he or she can rely on while at the same time begin on a lifetime of personal refinement of natural body movement that will continue to unfold as he or she progresses through all the stages of growing older.

Nagare

One of the fundamental principles emphasized in the Bujinkan dojo ninja training method is the concept of *nagare* (flowing) action. The idea of a flow refers equally to the movement from one action to the next, the body dynamics that deliver the movement, the physical logic that determines the appropriate movement, and the actual course of progress towards the desired outcome of the conflict.

For those students to whom the concept of nagare is foreign or even confusing, it is perhaps an effective educational device to reverse the concept and examine the results derived. Without an overall flowing quality, the student finds his or her moves to be unrelated single units quite independent structurally from other moves in the string of actions making up any given technique. Without flow, the student can often find himself struggling to force a technique to fit a situation that somehow seems

awkward, or find that the conflict has ended up in areas or shapes that had not been counted on. The absence of flowing grace forces fighting movements to rely on the muscle and bone power of the limbs alone, which is a dangerous habit for the student who could find him or herself the less stronger contender in a combat clash.

Ritsudo

Closely related to the quality of flowing adaptability is the concept of fitting in with or riding along with the *ritsudo* (rhythm) of the actions that make up the fight. This rhythm is an inherent part of any activity that involves the inter-related body dynamics of two or more individuals in motion. The rhythm of the actions of a conflict can also be described as the "breath" of the fight, as one phase leads into another in a back and forth of projecting and receiving that resembles the mechanics of breathing.

Ritsudo is an awareness of rhythm at several levels. At one level, the defender must fit in with the movements of his attacker in order to gain control of the direction of the fight. Another level of rhythm is characterized by the emotional fluctuations of both parties from second to second. Another rhythm is evidenced in the movements and muscular contractions that propel the bodies of the combatants. Perhaps ultimately, this ritsudo manifests itself as the progressing interplay of cause and effect in a fighting encounter. Your initial attack causes the effect of his angling back away with a counterstrike or grab which then becomes the cause of the effect of your attempting a follow-up lunge which is then the cause of his next move as an effect.... and the rhythm of the opposing forces continues until stillness is once again reached.

Total Training

In learning to handle a fighting situation well, and thereby ultimately learning how to transcend the limitations of needing to rely on physical defensive action, the student of the warrior ways can observe a triangular inter-relation of three major aspects of winning a conventional fight. Though each of the single aspects themselves could possibly be relied on as a total point of training focus, such narrow approaches will ultimately fall short when compared with total training.

Mechanics—the most efficient ways of moving the body in response to attacks; includes proper physical fundamentals such as footwork, angling and distancing, proper employment of body weapons, and effective techniques and strategies.

Dynamics—the most efficient means by which the mechanics are employed; includes proper applications of energy, rhythm and flow, strength and flexibility, speed relationships, and the ability to "feel and fit into" the action of the technique exchange.

Intention—the total commitment of the mechanics and dynamics towards the clearly recognized goal of victory; includes proper motivation for the application of violent methods, will to win that transcends normal fears or limits, and a mind-set that not only sees victory as the single possible outcome, but also has no concept of the possibility of losing.

As a means of training to apply this awareness of three-way interaction, the student can practice with two distinct methods of approach— training drills and fighting scenarios.

TRAINING DRILLS

Training drills isolate a particular movement, limb, or feeling and then allow the student to repeat the desired experience over and over again without concern for danger or the possibility of his or her technique being interrupted. Drills are purposely abstract, so that the student can concentrate on the piece of the action to be perfected without being distracted by the grander scope of what would happen in the totality of an actual fight. These abstract training drills allow the development of skills necessary for the application of techniques through the second training method of fighting scenarios.

Single Action Repetition

The trainee repeats a single action from a potential fighting response, working at eventual mastery through continuous experience. Again and again, the trainee works at blasting his training partner's at-

tacking arm out of its course towards him. (1-3) As the attacker lunges with a blow towards the face, (4) the trainee steps to the side, intercepting the attacking arm, (5) deflecting

Continued on following page

the blow, and (6) knocking the arm completely out of the way. (7) The exercise isolates and repeats the same attack with no attempt at follow-up or counter (8) as the attacker again

comes forward with a blow toward the face, (9) and the defender blocks it, (10) punches the attacker's arm, and (11) drives it out of the way.

Defense and Counter Repetition

Any given technique series can be practiced for perfection through drill. (1&2) As the attacker attacks, (3) his punch is knocked away with a strike to the arm, and then (4-7) the defender follows up with an open-hand strike to the neck. The attacker assists his defender by supplying the standard attack each time, and makes no attempt to trick or overthrow the response of the defender.

5

Strike and Defense Exchange

The defender and his attacker take turns exchanging an identical kicking attack and counter back and forth in continuous flowing succession. Strikes or punches could just as easily be drilled with this method. (1&2) As the attacker kicks, (3&4) the defender intercepts with his own leg, and kicks the attacking leg aside. (5&6) The defender in turn provides a counterkick to the other side, (7) which the attacker parries; (8-11) and the exchange is repeated over again.

1

Multiple Strike Succession Exchange

Both training partners take turns repeating an identical multiple-part flow of attacks and counters. As the attacker (1&2) leads with a left jab, (3&4) the defender knocks it away, then (5-8) parries another lunge punch to the

3

6

5

8

Continued on following page

9

face, (9-11) sweeps aside an uppercut by guiding it away from his body and (12&13) counters with his own body punch. (14-16) He immediately dives right back with the same attack pattern, this time as the aggressor, and the exchange continues on with the roles reversed.

11

14

Continued from preceding page

13

16

Grappling Flow Exchange

With a flow drill using a wrist twist as the technique to be perfected, both training partners take turns applying the throw and rolling out as a means of escape. Note that each time one of the partners is thrown, he retains control of the thrower's hand (as shown in the detail of step 4) by squeezing down on his fingers to hold him in place for the counterthrow. (1-2) The defender applies a wrist twist, and (3) throws the attacker. (4) The attacker, by squeezing down on the defender's hand to retain control and rolling (5) back up to a standing position, (6) reverses the situation by applying a wrist twist on the defender, and (7) the defender falls, (8) rolls out of the wrist twist, trapping the attacker's fingers in his hand, and (9) standing up, re-

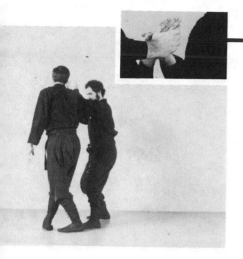

3

6

9

Continued on following page

10

Continued from preceding page

verses the hold. (10) The defender throws the attacker again. (11&12) The attacker rolls out of the wrist twist, retaining control of the defender's hand, and (13) comes back up to a standing position with the grip reversed. (14&15) He throws the defender on his back. (16&17) The defender rolls out of the wrist twist, and (18) reverses the hold on the attacker, and the procedure is repeated again.

13

16

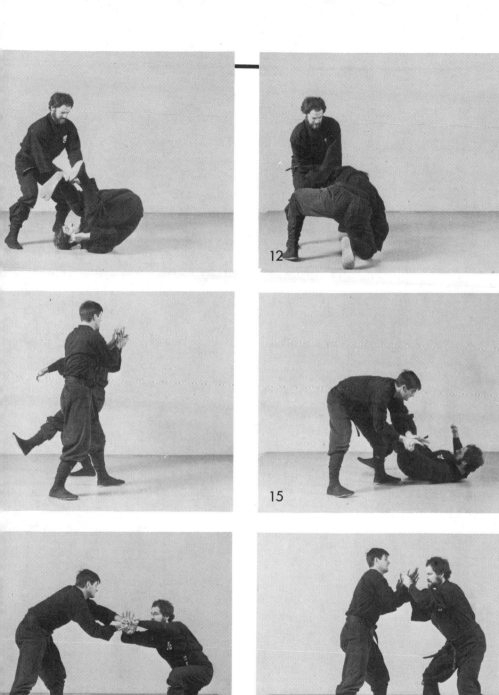

Weapon Grappling Flow Exchange

A continuous flow of grabs and throws uses the ninja's *hanbo* (cane). (1) The attacker thrusts, and (2) the defender steps to one side, and intercepts the attacker's lunge. Then (3-6) he uses arm and leg leverage to execute a defensive throw and disarm the attacker. (7) With roles now reversed,

5

Continued on following page

(8) the original defender becomes the attacker, and executes a thrust, (9) which the defender sidesteps and intercepts. (10-12) The defender then executes a defensive throw and disarms the new attacker. (13&14) The roles are again switched as the original attacker, now once again in possession of the hanbo executes a thrust, and the drill is repeated.

FIGHT SCENARIOS

The fight scenario recreates the fight in full detail, with accurately acted out body dynamics. Though fight scenarios can be drilled, and abstract drills can resemble the action of a fight, the two types of exercise serve different purposes.

Defense Against a Knife Lunge

(1&2) The attacker advances with a stab to the defender's midsection, which (3) the defender avoids with a last-second body shift and counterstrikes against the attacker's weapon hand. (4&5) The defender then continues with a punch to the ribs to unbalance his attacker, and then (6&7) a counterpunch against the attacker's

Continued on following page

Continued from preceding page

attempt to punch. (8&9) The defender then steps under the attacker's held arm while applying a rising forearm strike to the attacker's chin. (10&11) The defender's body movement provides the windup for a throw that stuns the attacker and (12&13) holds him in place for the defender's knee to the face and (14) disarm.

Flowing Action
in an Unarmed Defense

With motion flow, the defender, (1-3) avoids his attacker's punch. (4&5) The attacker grabs the defender's shoulder and (6&7) attempts a kick which (8&9) the defender blocks. (10&11) As the attacker then moves in

Continued on following page

with a punch, (12-17) the defender counters with attacks of his own to the limbs. (18) As the assault continues, the attacker manages to gain control once again and attempts (19) to throw the defender to finish the fight. The defender does not try to force the technique, but instead (20-22) goes along with the throw while securing the attacker's arm, using his rear body drop to propel the attacker's face into the ground and knocking him out.

Continued from preceding page

12

15

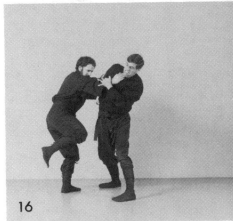

16

19

20

Body in Motion to Create Knockdown Power

(1-6) The defender uses her attacker's pull on her arm to propel her body forward with a shoulder slam to the upper arm of the attacker. (7) Her elbow lock arm bar holds the attacker in place for (8-10) a rear sweeping throw that forces the attacker face down to the ground. (11) The defender then stretches the attacker's arm between the top of one knee and the bottom of the other to create arm-breaking leverage.

4

8

Evasive Flowing Body Action with Counterblows

The defender evades his attacker's kicks and punches by means of flowing footwork and body angling, while simultaneously applying counterstrikes. (1-3) As the attacker kicks, (4) the defender steps to the side and (5) counters with a blow to the face. (6&7) The attacker's follow-up strike to the face (8&9) is sidestepped by the de-

Continued on following page

10

fender. (10&11) The defender punches the attacking arm out of the way. (12-15) The defender then grabs the attacker behind the ears, uses his thumbs to gouge the attacker's eyes, and (16-17) gaining a superior position by flipping him, (18) gouges his face with clawing hands.

13

16

Flowing from High to Low with Defensive Counters

On rough terrain, (1-3) the defender drops below his attacker's clubbing swing and (4&5) rises to punch the attacking arm, and again (6&7) drops low to avoid the attacker's roundhouse kick. (8) From his low vantage point, the defender moves in and (9) tackles the attacker's knee, and

Continued on following page

Continued from preceding page

(10&11) drives him down onto the ground. (12-14) To prevent the attacker from kicking with his free leg, the defender pulls back and down on the attacker's captured leg, dragging him across the surface of the rocks. (15-17) A sharp kick to the face and (18&19) a knee wrenching twist to the held leg then prevent the attacker from continuing the fight.

Flowing Along with a Technique Interruption

(1&2) The defender evades the attacker's leading hand punch by shifting back and to the inside with his entire body. (3&4) The defender then shifts to the inside of the stronger follow-up punch by the attacker while (5&6) executing a counterpunch to the attacker's exposed wrist. (7-10) A similar response then handles the third punch.

7

Continued on following page

Continued from preceding page

(11&12) The defender counterattacks with a *shikanken* (extended knuckle punch) into the shoulder joint and (13&14) a forearm slam into the side of the head, stunning the attacker and setting him up for (15-17) a shoulder damaging arm twist. (18) When the attacker attempts to pull out of the arm twist, (19&20) the defender goes with

Continued on following page

Continued from preceding page

that flow of action and follows along with a *kitenken* (hand edge strike) to the attacker's neck and then (21&22) a knee slam to the ribs. (23-25) As the attacker drops to the ground, the defender braces the extended arm and (26-28) steps across the falling body, (29&30) using his hips in motion to break the attacker's shoulder.

27

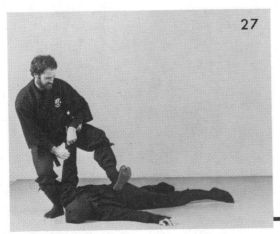

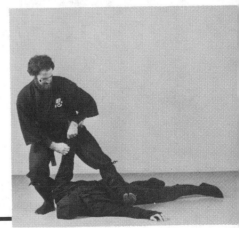

22

23

25

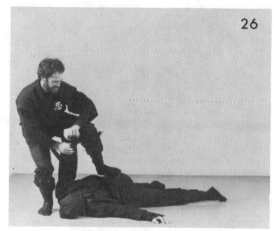

26

29

30

Use of Environment to Assist Flow

(1&2) The attacker stabs at the defender, who is up against a rock. (3) The defender fades inside the lunge and pulls him into (4) an elbow slam to the chin. (5-7) He steps under the attacker's arm and directs his head into the rock with an arm bar body slam. (8) He twists the attacker's arm with an arm lock and hits him with an elbow strike to the temple before (9-11) dropping his weight onto the attacker's leg to damage his knee and disarm him.

Arm Entrapping Defense

(1&2) The attacker grabs the defender to hold him in place for a punch to the face. (3) The defender slips to the inside of the punch while executing a distracting *shakoken* (palm-heel strike) to the underside of the attacker's jaw. (4-6) The defender then applies an arm bar and (7-9) a leg kick-out to force the adversary to the ground. Body weight pressure across the attacker's outstretched arm breaks his elbow.

Striking and Grappling Flow

(1-3) The attacker attempts a leading punch, which the defender knocks away with an outside clubbing strike. (4&5) The aggressor follows with a front kick. The defender evades to the outside, (6) with a simultaneous kick to the attacker's leg. (7&8) The attacker grabs the defender to pin him down. (9&10) The defender leaves the attacker's hand in place to facilitate a lunging *kitenken* (hand edge strike) to the neck. (11) Grabbing the attacker's

3

7

11

Continued on following page

Continued from preceding page

hand, (12&13) the defender then applies an *uragyaku* (inward wrist twist) to the attacker's trapped arm. (14&15) The attacker tries to free his hand, but (16) the defender flows right on to an *omotegyaku* (outward wrist twist) and (17&19) a hooking kick to knock the attacker down. (20-22) The defender then drops his weight on the bent wrist to damage the arm.

12

15

16

19

20

104

CHAPTER 4

KUNOICHI, THE DEADLY FLOWER

There are times when
yielding is power,
laughter is strength,
and a gentle touch is
the blow that subdues the assassin.
These too are great lessons
to be learned by even the mightiest of warriors.

The Japanese warlord Moritoki Mochizuki was killed in the famous battle of Kawanakajima in 1561, and his widowed wife Chiyome was left in the care and custody of her husband's uncle, the powerful Shingen Takeda. Rather than retire to the secluded life of a nun as might have been expected under the situation, Mochizuki's widow went on to play an active role in support of the great *daimyo* Takeda. At Takeda's request, Chiyome agreed to undertake the establishment of one of the most effective and yet undetected networks of *kunoichi* (female ninja) agents in the history of the Sengokujidai (Warring States Period) of Japan.

Shingen Takeda's idea was to have Chiyome Mochizuki set up a group of trained *miko* (female shrine attendants) who would act as spies, observers, and messengers throughout Takeda's Kai region (present-day

Yamanashi), as well as the Shinano territory (present-day Nigata) which was the prime target of conquest for both Shingen Takeda and his rival Kenshin Uesugi. Takeda had always made good use of ninja in his own domain as well as those of other lords. The kunoichi would be yet another means of gathering needed intelligence, or verifying reports from other sources and agents. The young female shrine attendants could easily travel around the area and interact with the local residents without arousing much suspicion at all, thereby adding to the overall strength of the Takeda family.

Chiyome established her underground academy in the village of Nazu, in Chiisa-gun of Shinshu (present-day Nagano), and went to work as the headmistress of her school for female ninja agents. Since the miko were always young unmarried girls, Chiyome Mochizuki began recruiting appropriate candidates from the ranks of the countless children rendered homeless by the all-consuming civil war that raged throughout the island nation of Japan. Takeda's kunoichi trainer became foster mother to any orphaned, abandoned, runaway, or lost girls who found themselves in the Shinshu region without anyone to turn to. To the citizens of the region, Chiyome appeared to be nothing more than a kindly compassionate woman who was working to provide some comfort and spiritual value to the lives of certain young girls who would have otherwise been relegated to a life of misery and wretchedness.

The girls were instructed in the duties, manners, and knowledge of the miko vestal virgins who served the priests of the Shinto shrines of the land. In addition to the standard training, however, the young charges of Chiyome Mochizuki were also given a thorough grounding in a mind-set perception that would later guarantee their loyalty in all situations. By continuously prompting and reminding the girls of the source of their salvation from a life of misery, Chiyome worked to bind the girls to her. The girls were encouraged to examine their previous lives over and over in the same way. What had led them to their misery? Who let them down? Who found them and saved them when all seemed lost? The girls eventually came to believe that the only way to survive in the world was to depend on their strong ties with their fellow sisters from the academy and to demonstrate total loyalty to Chiyome Mochizuki.

As a third step in the girls' education, Chiyome taught them how to obtain information valuable to her, how to analyze and evaluate situations, how to cause confusion and dissention through the planting of rumors, how to recruit reliable messengers who could pass on information to other kunoichi miko in the network, how to disguise themselves,

and how to use their feminine charm to manipulate men when appropriate. Once completing the course of indoctrination and training at the ninja academy in Nazu village, the girls were sent out to become a part of Chiyome Mochizuki's female agent group.

Chiyome gathered her intelligence from all over the two target provinces, also picking up knowledge from travelers who had journeyed in from outlying areas, and passed her findings on to Shingen Takeda directly. To protect the efficiency and integrity of the kunoichi ring, Chiyome Mochizuki's role in Takeda's scheme was disclosed to nobody, and remained a secret for the life of the great general.

The history of feudal Japan is filled with such stories as that of the female ninja of Koga ryu's Mochizuki family. All members of the family were ready to do whatever was required to ensure the security and safety of their clan, women as well as men, and each person had his or her roles and specialties. Women could often move undetected and unsuspected in circles where male agents would find it difficult or impossible to fit in, which made them especially valuable for purposes of espionage that would better enhance the family's chances for survival.

Kunoichi Training

Historically, the kunoichi was trained in a manner similar to her male counterparts, although the instruction of the female ninja did emphasize the more subtle aspects of personal one-on-one warfare. Small unit battlefield tactics that would be taught to her brothers would have been less important than skills of psychology and the manipulation of another's personality or perspective through behavior modification, and the channeling of her intuition, all of which were emphasized in the historical kunoichi training. The preparation of kunoichi for active field work did of course include basic instruction in the ninjutsu combat methods of *taijutsu* (unarmed self-protection), *bojutsu* and *hanbojutsu* (staff and cane fighting), *tantojutsu* (knife techniques), *yarijutsu* (spear usage), and *ninpo kenjutsu* (sword methods). The tactics, however, were designed to fit the specific situation of a smaller female contending with and escaping from larger male adversaries, rather than situations of commando-type attacks against guard positions or sentry outposts.

This same emphasis on pragmatic approaches toward using the body's structure and dynamics in a scientific manner continues to guide the training of current-day female members of the authentic Japanese ninjutsu tradition. With a working ability to apply the principles of naturalness of motion and adaptability to the elements of the situation through taijutsu, female practitioners of the shinobi art can use their generally smaller stature and natural grace to successfully handle any life-threatening or potentially injurious situation. As with all other aspects of ninjutsu, what more conventional thinkers would label as "weaknesses," the ninja sees as tools.

Accommodations must of course be made for the realities of female self-protection in the current age, just as was true in eras past. Footwork dynamics must be adjusted to the normal daily dress and footwear of the female practitioner. Skirts and dresses that wrap around the legs in a binding manner and shoes with straps or elevated soles pose the same

problems that wraparound kimonos and *zori* (slip-on sandals) and *geta* (wooden clogs) once created for the historical female ninja. Strength ratios between average female defenders and male attackers must also be acknowledged, rendering self-defense tactics that rely on power punching, kicking, or throwing virtually useless in realistic life-threatening encounters.

Another crucial aspect of self-protection for female ninja is the woman's potential for employing what seem to be brutal tactics against a fellow human being. In the contemporary Western world, just as it was in ancient Japan, female members of society are subtlely taught that their demeanors ought to be gentle and refined. Stereotypically, little boys are taught to be tough and competitive on the sports field, while little girls are taught to be accommodating and sociable in the home. From ancient history right up to today, males have generally been regarded as the contending breadwinners, while females have generally been regarded as the appeasing peacemakers. This cultural or perhaps biological-hormonal orientation towards uniting tendencies can often interfere with the realization that a life threat from an attacker has materialized in all its malevolent darkness. Unfortunately, all too often it takes the civilized victim, whether female or male, too long to come to the realization that the attack is indeed real, and that protective action is demanded. That deadly hesitation for the thought, "It really is happening to me!" to pass through the conscious mind is all it takes for the attacker to gain complete control of the situation.

The teachings of the historical Togakure ryu ninjutsu tradition recognize a dangerous attacker as having given up the right to be regarded as a sentient being worthy of loving consideration, and suggest that such attackers be regarded as non-human demonic forces or crazed savage animals that must be dealt with by any means required for a successful outcome to the unfortunate encounter. They have relinquished the right to be considered as human by means of their descent into inhuman behavior. Just as any human body is capable of producing healthy cells that ensure the growth of the body, as well as deadly cancerous cells that threaten to destroy the body if unchecked, the greater part of humankind seems to produce its own images of "growth" and "cancer" beings. Each such being must be recognized for its inherent value and handled with appropriate means. Any person considering himself or herself worthy of living a happy and healthy life of meaning must realize the deadly folly of regarding dangerous killers and maimers as fellow humans worthy of consideration. Such vicious entities are "fellow" only to other such cancerous beings.

Nin-po Taijutsu Methods of Kunoichi

The following examples show a few of the nin-po taijutsu methods appropriate for one of smaller stature, of less relative strength, occasionally wearing restrictive clothing—typical in a situation where the female ninja must contend with a larger male assailant.

Defense Against a Rear Arm Choke

(1) In this example of Bujinkan dojo nin-po taijutsu training for women, the defender is attacked from behind by an assailant who applies a rear forearm choke to cut off her air and pull her backwards onto the ground. (2&3) She responds by stabbing backwards over her shoulder with her straightened fingers to distract her attacker from the pressure of his choke. (4) As the attacker reaches up to move the defender's hand away from his eyes, (5) the defender uses the moment to

2

4

5

Continued on following page

shift her body into a more stable position. (6&7) She immediately lowers her weight down and back onto the attacker's extended leg, (8) either breaking the knee or forcing the attacker to the ground. (9-11) The defender then shifts her body weight behind an elbow arm bar in order to drive her attacker's face into the ground.

7

8

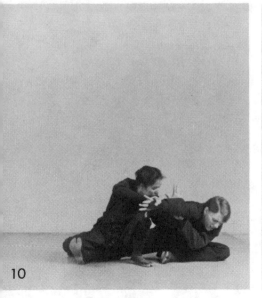

10

11

Knife Retention in a Clash

(1&2) A stronger attacker attempts to wrest away the knife that the defender has taken up in her defense. His greater strength prevents her from employing any sort of wrist leverage move, and her kimono prevents her from freeing her leg for any sort of kicking defense. (3) The defender allows her arm to be held in place and shifts her hips back and down with a crouching pivot away from her own knife. (4) This action causes the knife to cut across the attacker's wrist without the defender having to apply any great power, and at the same time, takes her out of range of any possible retaliatory kicks. Again shifting laterally on crouching knees, she moves across her attacker to capture his power and continues to direct his movements in such a manner that he cannot get to her. (5) As the defender moves, she allows the back of her blade to capture the attacker's wrist while she pulls back and across with her body weight in motion for power, slamming her elbow into the attacker's temple. (8&9) A palm-heel strike directing her body weight into the back of the attacker's outstretched arm breaks his elbow and forces him to the ground in submission.

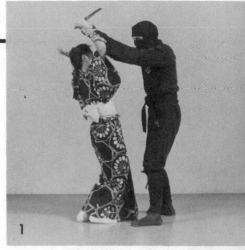

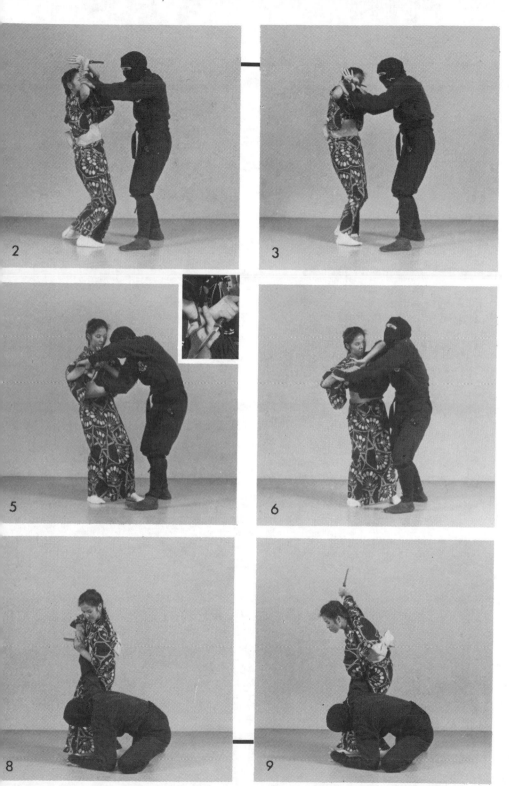

2

3

5

6

8

9

Defense Against Wrist Restraint and Choke

(1-3) The attacker has grabbed the female defender by the wrist and throat in an attempt to choke her. (4-8) Rather than resist his strength and leverage as he might have expected, the defender charges in with an *urashuto kitenken* (knife-edge hand attack) to the attacker's throat, using her assailant's pulling motion to her own advantage. The nin-po taijutsu shuto strike uses the thumb to brace the extended fingers for more support, allowing the hand increased strength. Unlike the conventional straight-fingered "judo chop" as shown in most self-defense books, the ninja's *kitenken* (angled-finger strike) pops open from a closed fist upon impact with

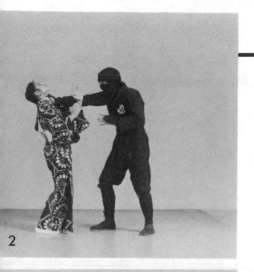

2

4

5

7

8

Continued on following page

9

the target. (9) The defender then takes advantage of the momentarily stunning blow to free her arm from the attacker's gripping hand (10) and moves her body into position for relief of the choke. (11-14) The defender then pivots back towards the attacker while punching up into the underside of his arm and peeling his weakened hand loose. (15&16) A rising forearm strike to the attacker's groin then knocks him back and away to allow her to escape.

11

14

10

12

13

15

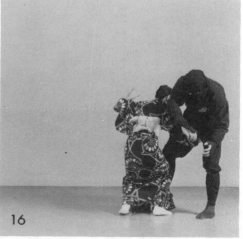

16

Defense Against a
Wrist Restraint and Slap

(1&2) The female defender is held in place by her male attacker, who holds both of her smaller wrists in his larger hand and slaps across and down at her face. (3) She responds by leaving her wrists in place while dropping around to the side of the assailant's gripping arm to avoid the strike. (4-6) Once in place behind her attacker, the defender slams her knee into the back of the enemy's knee with a sinking

2

3

5

6

Continued on following page

Continued from preceding page

7

leverage action, (7) forcing him to the ground in an effortless manner. The defender allows her back to remain erect so that the attacker will have to release his hands to break his fall rather than hit his face or shoulder on the floor. (8-12) The female defender immediately follows up her escape with a swinging shin kick to the attacker's face.

10

Hanbo Defense Against a Roundhouse Kick

(1) The defender confronts an assailant with her *hanbo* (cane) poised for a strike. (2&3) The attacker attempts to avoid the cane by using his superior size and reach in a karate-style roundhouse kick. (4) Rather than resist the shock of the impact, the defender drifts in towards her attacker's center with a cane tip strike to the underside of her assailant's chin, eluding the kick. (5) She then lifts the trailing end of the cane from beneath the kicker's extended leg (6&7) to topple him with assistance from a footsweep. (8) Forward binding pressure from the cane then damages the attacker's leg to prevent him from regaining his footing to continue the fight.

2

4

5

7

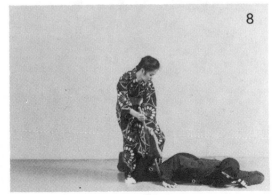

8

Defense from Against the Wall

(1) The defender is restrained by both wrists and shoved toward a wall. (2) In response, she lowers her hips and quickly pulls her leg up to aim at the assailant's rear leg, (3&4) which she knocks out with a forward heel stomp kick. (5) As the attacker falls forward, the defender meets his face with *shakoken* (palm-heel strikes) to the jaw, (6) which turn into thumbnail rips along the attacker's upper gums and

2

3

5

6

Continued on following page

Continued from preceding page

then (7&8) a two-handed thumb hook tearing action across the assailant's mouth. As the enraged attacker lifts his head to relieve the pain, the female defender executes a *zutsuki* (forehead smash) into his nose and upper lip. It is important to note that the head smash action is derived from the entire body in motion, and not a mere nodding snap from the neck muscles. (9) The defender then plants her foot on top of the attacker's leading foot to pin it in place, (10) and uses a knee ram action against the attacker's immobilized knee (11&12) to topple him with a fall that will cause his pinned ankle to break.

7

10

8

9

11

12

Defense Against a Body Pin

(1-3) The defender is restrained with a tackling action that works to hold her in place. (4&5) Bracing the attacker's head with one hand, she uses her other hand to apply a fingernail cutting action (6) into the cartilage folds in the attacker's ear. (7) As the assailant lifts his head in response to the pain, (8&9) he is met with an elbow

3

6

9

Continued on following page

10

Continued from preceding page

smash to the temple. (10-14) The defender then pulls back against the bone and cartilage of the nose with finger hooking action to expose the attacker's throat (15-17) for a hand edge strike that collapses the assailant's windpipe, (18) and knocks him to the ground.

13

16

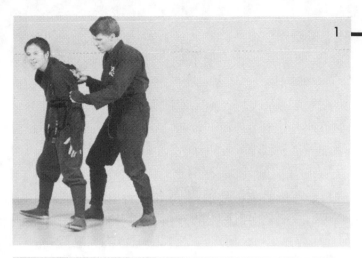

Defense Against an Arm Twist

(1) An attacker grabs the defender and twists her arm up behind her back in an effort to control and direct her. (2) She shifts forward with the foot on the side of the twisted arm to relieve the pressure by altering the angle, as well as pull the attacker off balance. (Note that this move would probably be appropriate only for persons with sufficient training in the ninja's *junan taiso* (warm up exercises) limbering methods or some other yoga-like system that emphasizes suppleness of the body. Self-protection

begins with good health.)
(3) The defender suddenly shifts her body in the opposite direction, trapping the attacker's guiding arm by lifting what was her trailing hand. (4) She then leans forward with a crouching shift of her knee against the attacker's leg, damaging his knee, and (5) taking him to the ground with the twisting pressure of her body weight against his trapped leg. (6) Once the attacker is down, the defender now has the advantage. Keeping her eyes on the attacker at all times,

Continued on following page

7

8

(7) the defender stands up, (8) steps in just as the attacker is about to try to recover, (9) raises her leg before he has a chance to do anything, and (10) executes a heel stomp kick to

9

10

11

the attacker's face. (11) making sure to follow through on the blow for maximum effectiveness, and (12) puts an end to the struggle.

12

Defense Against a Two-Handed Choke

(1&2) The attacker grabs the defender in an attempt to choke off her breathing. (3) She responds by dropping the point of her knee onto the bridge of the attacker's leading foot, bringing all her weight down to damage the small bones beneath her knee. (4-6) The defender then uses her head to strike against the underside of the assailant's arm as she rises and moves to the outside of the attacker's reach. (7) A ramming knee strike then

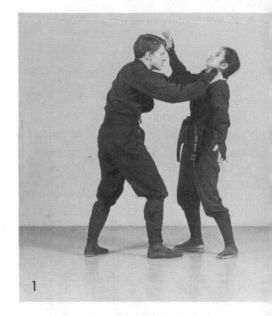

1

4

5

2

3

6

7

Continued on following page

Continued from preceding page

8

(8) stuns the attacker's leg to prevent him from readily following the defender's escape. (9) The defender then plants her foot behind the attacker's weakened leg, (10) and uses clawing fingers to grab the attacker's hair and lower lip (11-14) for a throw onto his back.

11

12

CHAPTER 5

THE FORCE OF INTENTION

When the true seeker of wisdom
  hears of the mysterious powers of the shinobi warriors,
  he feels compelled to study them actively.
When the ordinary man hears of those teachings,
  he discusses them with other intellects.
When the idiot hears of the teachings,
  he smirks and laughs and shakes his head.

Many of the ancient legends concerning the historical ninja of feudal Japan are woven around tales of ninjutsu's incredible mystical powers that supposedly afforded the night warriors of Iga and Koga Provinces vast capabilities far beyond the conventional fighters of the time. Various other martial arts in addition to ninjutsu are also said to employ mysterious qualities that seem to transcend the mundane limits of the physical realm. Tales of internal powers *(ki, chi)*, and universal forces are indeed inspiring and fascinating to many martial artists today.

Unfortunately, for all too many martial artists it is often true that the search for supernormal forces is actually a symptom of a seeker's refusal to accept his or her birth-given role in physical reality. If there were some sort of "force" that could come down into our bodies to make us invulnerable, then we could effortlessly gain control over our world without having to do any work or make any investment in effort, it might be stated. The shortcut does sound tempting, and is alluring to many, but ultimately cannot exist independently of the physical.

If indeed there is any sort of "mysterious force" that can be utilized by the common man or woman to enhance combat capabilities, its source will undoubtedly be found in the hard realities of the physical dimension. Only by first cultivating and working your way through a firm understanding of how your own body and its energies operate, relate with others, and create new realities can you ever hope to attain the keys to transcending the physical realm. As attractive as the seemingly cosmic methods may be, it is impossible to gain any control over the mental, let alone the spiritual, realms of power without first honestly coming to grips with all the aspects of our "physicalness." Unfortunately, this reality is often ignored or repressed in the methods of many martial, religious, and intellectual systems.

It should be noted that there is indeed a realm of power that somehow lies accessible beyond the normal physical skills. This reality is often overlooked by a vast majority of contemporary martial artists who struggle on with the hopeless futility of relying on crude bone and muscle speed and strength despite the obvious warnings of advancing age. The point being emphasized here, however, is the fact that this supraphysical ability cannot be studied as a system of training in and of itself without first gaining competency in the physical techniques that make up the ninja's combat art. Just as you cannot get to work on the fifth story of a building without first constructing a foundation and the first four floors, diving into a study of spiritual power or ethereal forces without a firm foundation and internalized experience in physical training is merely putting off a cold reality that must eventually be faced.

Progressively Expanding Awareness

As an initial point of awareness when first exploring the possibility of there being something "beyond technique," it should be noted that one of the most difficult aspects of developing true skill in the ninja warrior arts is the ability to let go of personal individual focus when it is necessary to be more in touch with a broader range of influencing factors. The new student is primarily concerned with the performance of his or her own mechanical defensive movements, and often finds it difficult to concentrate on, or even see, anything beyond immediate arm's reach. As years of training experiences accumulate, however, it becomes easier and easier for the student to relax his or her focus of attention and expand the awareness to take in more and more of the subtle factors that influence the potential outcome of any given conflict or confrontation.

The development of fighting skill in the ninja combat arts could be seen as a process of progressing through several distinct stages. Each stage is a level of ability that opens up even more possibilities for the student practitioner. These stages are in no way set with boundaries or degree licenses, nor are they easily definable with clearly marked points of transition. Instead, they can be seen to overlap considerably, and in reality can be recognized only after several have been grown through to the point where they can be looked back upon.

First Stage

The first stage is best defined as one of concentration on your own physical capabilities. During this training period, strong emphasis is placed on learning the fundamental principles of the ninjutsu armed and unarmed combat methods with an eye towards gaining personal proficiency in the body skills that make up the *kihongata* (basic foundation) of the art. This stage is a time to focus on the way your body picks up, adapts and adapts to, and learns to perform all the mechanical aspects of getting a solid grounding in the art. Though effective self-protection is ever a concern of personal development in the ninja combat method, this first stage of training is a time to pay particular attention to how your body is operating and how much your body is capable of. There is less emphasis on being expected to generate specific results in relation to the varied moves an attacker could execute against you.

Second Stage

The second stage is best defined as one of concentration on your responsive relationship with an attacker and his advances against you. Once you have developed a reasonable level of skill in performing the mechanical fundamental movements of the art to the point where you can deliver kicks, throws, strikes, cuts, and so forth, with confidence in their effectiveness, you next begin to focus on applying those movement principles in response against an attacker. This stage is a time to focus on the distancing, spontaneous decision making, and fitting in with an attacker's techniques that will make your techniques effective and ultimately superior. Proper response that facilitates effortless countertechnique is the goal of this stage of personal development in the ninja combat arts.

Third Stage

The third stage is best defined as one of concentration on your ability to control and direct the total energy of the conflict. Once you have developed familiarity with the mechanical pieces of the art, and then have cultivated the skills of applying them scientifically against another's movements, it is time to focus on developing your ability to cause your assailant to have to do things in a manner that will prove to be to your benefit at his expense. Concepts of attacker and defender and assault and counter fade at this point. The fight somehow is no longer perceived as a contending between two or more independent units, but rather comes to be experienced as a single unit of give and take energy in continuous flow. You can at this point transcend the level of relating to an aggressor's movements with your own movements. As subject and object blend, you in essence become one with the energy of the fight.

Fourth Stage

The fourth stage is best defined as one of concentration on your ability to conceal yourself safely in the very center of the energy of the fight, thereby disappearing from the threat of danger by slipping into the middle of it. Difficult if not impossible to describe effectively through the written word, this stage of development allows you to transcend the conventional principles and strategies for dealing with combat situations. In this fourth stage, you enter a realm where you can create the impression of certain kinds of energies, only to "break the rules" and defy seeming logic in order to overcome an assailant. The anti-principles of *kyojitsu tenkan ho* (the method of altering the perception of truth and falsehood) provide the insights necessary to take you to an ability level where slowness can be seen to overcome speed, weakness can be seen to defeat strength, gentleness can be seen to crush force, and staying in the path of an attack can be seen to provide escape from vulnerability.

Void Realm

Those few rare individuals who continue their training quest long enough to go on beyond these four roughly categorized successive levels of personal development then enter into the vast range of freedom and effortless power experienced as the *ku no seikai* (realm devoid of specific recognizeable manifestation). Mysterious and perplexing beyond description, and perhaps even terrifying to the uninitiated observer outside of the tradition, this void realm is not really a fifth stage as such, but rather a complete leaving behind of so-called "stages" altogether. It is at this level where the warrior seems to become a wizard, capable of transcending and leaving behind the conventional limitations and appearances of the martial arts as most practitioners know them.

To the consternation of many Western world students, there is no way to shortcut the process and go directly to the higher powers of the spiritual warrior. Exercises in ki power, flow sensitivities, chi storing and such without the benefit of first developing reliable skill in hands-on physical combat methods are as pointless as establishing corporate marketing strategy without first deciding on what type of product the company will produce.

There are however a variety of exercises that can provide a brief look at some of the budding refinements of higher skill once the physical fundamentals begin to be internalized. Though these exercises in no way replace or supersede the need for diligent and disciplined training in the authentic and proven physical methods of the warrior arts, they can provide an idea of the type of awareness to which the maturation of physical skill could eventually lead.

EXERCISE ONE

Blending with an Opponent's Efforts

To develop a sense of the energy involved in tuning into and blending with an adversary's moving attempts to gain control over the fight, students can practice a form of pre-set clash spontaneity in which one given technique is executed successfully and then rerun in a manner that permits the original victim to reverse the outcome.

The initial techniques used in this type of training should be fairly simple and direct in order to give a firm sense of effectiveness. That way, it is easier to feel the natural direction in which the attack is leading in order to better grasp the concept of how to "ride" the attack as a means of overcoming it.

Technique Reversal

(1&2) The attacker steps forward with a straight punch at the face or up-raised hands of the defender. The defender counters by allowing his body to slip to the outside of the attacker's punching arm. (3-5) Once removed from danger, the defender can then counter with a step-

through lunging punch to the attacker's upper ribs. In the advanced application of this technique, the side slip and counterpunch are blended together to remove the "one-two" timing and streamline the action into a single slip and counterpunch move.

Technique Reversal Turnaround

(1&2) The attacker steps in as before, and the defender attempts the identical counter. (3) This time however, the initial attacker perceives the punch coming in and allows his body to fade to the outside of the punching arm. The attacker's free trailing hand can also subtlely re-

4

5

direct the counter at the same time if necessary. (4-6) As the attacker continues forward with the momentum of his initial punch, he transforms his straightline movement into an angled elbow strike as a means of successfully going after the repositioned target.

6

EXERCISE TWO

Subtle Energies

As a means of gaining more experience in the subtle energies involved in an attack contention situation, the students can practice a form of slow motion perception movement that can give the idea of what is meant by a fight being one unit of give and take energy, as opposed to two independent energy units bouncing off of each other with no relationship whatsoever. The object of the exercise is to attain the feeling of single unit action, and not at all to compete with the training partner or in any way attempt to fool or throw him or her off.

To begin the exercise, take several minutes to properly warm up. In addition to standard basic energy stimulating calisthenics such as pushups and brisk running, special attention should be paid to the hands. Then, as you do the exercise, be sure to breathe deeply and regularly, being aware of increasing energy with each incoming breath, and the release of inhibiting factors with each outgoing breath. Explore the energy between your hands.

The in and out breathing process and the building and releasing of the body's energy field follows a positive and negative charging cycle that is captured in the Oriental *in* and *yo* in which all extremes of polarity are seen to reverse themselves eventually. This exercise gives the advanced student a direct experience of the relative nature of attack and defense energies. Which is the attacker: the student pulling the other student's energy along, or the student pushing away the other student's energy?

1

Warm Up for Energy Sensitivity Exercise

(1-5) Begin by shaking out the arms and hands vigorously to increase the blood circulation and tactile awareness. (6-8) After a few moments of shaking out, pull your hands up in front of your chest palm to palm without allowing them to touch. See how far apart you can pull them while still feeling the increased warmth between them. Slowly push and pull the

4

2

3

5

6

Continued on following page

Continued from preceding page

7

hands together and apart, and then (9-12) begin to rotate them slightly against each other in a circular manner. Notice the sensations of heat, proximity, electromagnetic attraction or repulsion, and any other outstanding sensations previously unnoticed. See if you can feel an imaginary ball of this energy rolling between your palms.

10

Energy Sensitivity Exercise

(1-11) Maintain your heightened electromagnetic energy awareness, and move into position in front of your training partner with your hands still in front of your chest. Bring your hands together to the point where you can begin to feel the other person's energy. Explore this energy by checking how far apart your hands can be and still feel some connection. Gradually begin to move slowly, checking how advancing pressure can

2

4

5

Continued on following page

Continued from preceding page

6

be felt to move your hand back, and re-treating pull can be felt to move your hand forward. With your knees flexed comfortably, see if the hand energy awareness alone can be felt to direct your movements as you very slowly allow yourself to flow with the subtle currents. In more advanced stages of this exercise, both training partners can close their eyes to add to the subtlety of the perception required.

9

7

8

10

11

EXERCISE THREE

Drifting Just Beyond Reach

As an extremely advanced method of training to handle long-range speed punches that cannot be knocked aside or countered, a system of "riding" the expanding energy of a punch can be practiced for proficiency. Rather than leap far to the side or attempt to reach up and down with blocking actions, the skillful fighter can drift in the direction of the force of the punch in a manner that permits the punching arm to travel unhindered at the target, and yet always be just a shade short of impact with the target. This action is not a boxer's duck or weave, but rather a complete body movement away from the damage of the punch (or kick). By remaining just close enough to be missed barely, or even touched with

non-damaging results, the superior fighter allows his or her adversary to think that their strike is effective and on target. This encourages the adversary to continue to commit him or herself to a punch that is useless, rather than withdraw or redirect due to the perception that the punch will not work as thrown.

The exercise should be performed with the minimum of speed in the beginning. Take the time to get to know the flexibility possible within the factors of distance, timing, and relative speed. Only after sufficient training at extremely slow speeds should you even consider practicing at real fight tempo.

Riding the Expanding Energy of an Attempted Strike

In this example, (1-5) the attacking training partner advances with a leading hand shot to the face of the defender, who drifts back as the punch approaches his face. The defender rides the expanding energy of the punch to remain as a target throughout the ac-

tion, but just beyond the reach of the attacker's punch. The defender employs all his perceptive skills in judging his physical relationship to the approaching blow. (6) The attacker then begins a cross punch to the midsection,

Continued on following page

7

8

which (7-9) the defender evades in the same manner. Next, (10-12) the attacker follows up with another leading hand shot to the face which is again evaded. Of course, any punch or kick combination could be used for training.

9

With each punch, the defending training partner fades back with knee and hip gliding action to keep the target right where the attacker will expect it to be, and yet just the smallest distance out of range.

EXERCISE FOUR

The Proper Approach to Training

Whenever engaging in any exchange of set techniques with a training partner, remember to allow several repetitions of the drill or fight scenario for "combat feeling intensity," along with routine distance and timing work. All too often, the work of developing the technical aspects of a given action can overshadow the realization that if you were to apply the technique in question in actual life or death combat, your own commitment to a winning outcome would constitute the major deciding factor in the results. Beware the danger of playing around with fighting techniques in so-called "sparring," where a succession of flicking, pecking darts and stings are ventured out and back with a great deal of preliminary footwork, bouncing, or unnecessarily close body positioning which continuously produces tension.

Use your imagination when training with a fellow practitioner. Certainly you want to enjoy your training session, but do not drift into the negative habit of relying on cleverness or complex technique strings alone. Concentrate on the feeling. How would you be handling yourself and the situation if every move could lead to your disfigurement or death? Pay attention to details and be there in the imaginary fight 100 percent.

Though many conventional martial artists would perhaps argue the point, the truth is that five minutes of intense full-awareness technique exchanging is far preferable to 20 minutes of drawn-out sparring, if actual combat fighting ability is the desired goal. You can always run or do cross-country walking for aerobic conditioning later. Do not make the deadly mistake of watering down your combat training for the sake of indulging yourself in "a good workout."

EXERCISE FIVE

Sensing the Power of Intention

It is sometimes possible for the experienced warrior to experience the power of directed intentions through the action of the senses operating on a more subtle level than normal. Though one can not train for this ability alone without progressing through countless hours of experience in eye to eye clash situations, it is sometimes possible for an advanced student to experience the feeling in the remote almost non-physical sense through various training exercises.

Perceiving Intention

Several students, one a stalker and the rest receivers, position themselves so that the receivers are in a circle with their eyes closed and their backs turned in towards the stalker, who stands in center position in the middle of the ring. (1) The stalker chooses one of the receivers as the "victim," and concentrates intently on moving up behind him or her with an attack. (2) The stalker takes as much time as desired. The waiting receivers relax and allow themselves to be aware of any impressions that come to them. Sounds, moving air, and even heat at close range, could all be possible cues. (3) The stalker approaches his victim and (4) brings his hands up and around the receiver's neck to simulate a strangle. (5) If the receiver feels the stalker moving up behind, he or she can raise one hand to indicate the impression that the stalker is there. (6) If the stalker is indeed about to pounce on that receiver, a touch of the stalker's hand on the receiver's upraised hand tells him or her that the impression was true. If the wrong receiver lifts a hand prompted by an incorrect hunch, there will be no stalker there to touch it, and therefore the receiver will know to lower the hand after a few moments of no feedback. The receiver who fails to notice the stalker and therefore gets caught becomes the new stalker for a new round of the game. It should be emphasized that for the training exercise to be effective, the stalker must concentrate intently on his or her objective, for indeed it is a concentration exercise. While moving as silently as possible, the stalker pours forth intention in an attempt to arouse the receiver's attention.

AFTERWORD

An interview with Stephen Hayes

The following interview with Shidoshi Stephen K. Hayes, author of Ohara Publications' ninja book series, has been included in this volume to offer readers further insight into the work of the author and the significance of his art. The rather pointed questions and their answers have been compiled from several separate discussion forums conducted by the shidoshi at his seminars and camps held throughout the Western world. —Ed.

Q. *How did you come to set up your homes in places like the countryside of Ohio in the United States and rural Kumamoto in Japan? Wouldn't there be more interest in your art in the major cities on the East or West Coasts of America?*
A. I wanted areas where I could be surrounded by a healthy environment. We have our own water supply. The soil is good for growing our

own food. Plenty of firewood for winters. Closeness with nature has always been a major aspect of the ninja lifestyle, and it is the same today.

Q. *Isn't it difficult finding students in the remote places you live?*

A. Students have to find us, not the other way around. If it is a little difficult to get to us, only the most sincere will make it. This is too rich a warrior art for the masses. I would not want to be teaching people who were coming to my training hall out of mere convenience.

Q. *How many people actually go through the personal difficulty of moving to where you are teaching, just to get involved with the art?*

A. Numbers are not really that important, especially when you consider how much publicity the art has received since 1980. However, I can say that we always have more than enough students to fill our training hall. They come from all over the United States, as well as from other nations.

Q. *Do the students all live together with you at the school?*

A. No. That would not be in keeping with the true essence of the warrior tradition. We are not a cult or commune where the student can find shelter from the real world. We insist that our students live in and be part of the greater community in which the dojo is located. I believe that successfully making it in real life is actually a part of ninja training.

---

*"I suppose I would have to say that
I'm a traditionalist, in that my warrior tradition
stretches back over 1,300 years
of Japanese history."*

Q. *Is it possible that ninjutsu has become too commercialized today?*

A. If anything, I would have to say that the art is undercommercialized. Despite all the business possibilities that might lie waiting out there, the authentic art as taught in my training halls is still very difficult to find and attain licensing in. The student has to earn his or her way into the life art of nin-po. You will not find chains of Stephen Hayes ninja school franchises.

What has been overcommercialized in the Western world are all the trappings of the art, those elements that have little to do with with the essence of the true ninja warrior tradition—silly gimmicks, made up weapons, and fantasyland costumes, totally inaccurate ninja films and shows, in which the beauty and power of my art is misrepresented. Publishers also have poured out countless ninjutsu books and magazines authored by persons posing as teachers who have had absolutely no training in the art whatsoever. Perhaps these aspects are what are referred to when people talk of commercialization. These things have nothing to do with the reality of ninjutsu.

Q. *With your background of professional acting and stunt work in Japan, and your obvious reputation as being the only American really qualified to serve as a technical director for a ninja film, it is shocking to hear that you have never played a part in any of the several ninja movies or TV shows that have come out in the past few years. Why is this?*

A. I was invited to work with a few film companies on their so-called ninja productions, but when I investigated the scripts and story lines, I found that what the producers and marketing people wanted a ninja to be had little to do with the reality I was working to teach. I would have been embarrassed to have my teacher see me in something that degraded the precious art that he shared with me. True ninjutsu has yet to appear on any movie or TV screen in the Western world as of the time of this interview.

Q. *Would you work with a production crew if they were doing a film that portrayed ninjutsu as you think it should be interpreted?*

A. If my schedule permitted it, yes. I think that would help the maligned image of my art greatly. Someday there will be a producer who will want to go beyond the silly stereotyping of ninjutsu in the marial arts film as we know it and bring out something that shows the full potential of all the facets of the ninja warrior tradition.

Q. *As a martial artist, do you think of yourself as a traditionalist or a modernist?*

A. Actually, thinking in terms of labels like that is a restricting habit I like to avoid. If forced to choose one term, however, I suppose I would have to say that I am a traditionalist, in that my warrior tradition stretches back over 1,300 years of Japanese history. You can not get much more traditional than that. On the other hand, I could be seen as a modernist, in that one of the most important traditions of nin-po is to think modernly, with state-of-the-art awareness. That keeps ninjutsu from becoming an outmoded antique. Therefore, in the true spirit of the art, the most traditional thing I can do is to keep on training in modern clothing, in realistic surroundings, and contemporary situations.

Q. *Why do you feel it is so important to emphasize the fact that your warrior tradition has gone through so many generations of history?*

A. History validates an art through the tests of time and successful results. The past generations of our ryu were forced by conditions of the economic, political, and military environment to develop a real system of combat survival that worked every time. People acutally lived or died, based on the system's effectiveness. There was no room for idle or fanciful theory. If a technique did not work, it died on the battlefield, so there was no way that something less than effective could be brought back and included in the ever-growing body of knowledge being developed by the members of the ryu.

Q. *Couldn't marital artists today do the same sort of research, and develop their own ninjutsu systems?*

A. No, that is not possible. Where today are we going to get the opportunity to actually test out the damaging or killing techniques of any new theoretical system that we might invent? We would have to leave behind a virtual mountain of corpses as a result of our tests with fists, blades, and sticks if we were to validate our theories through the actual testing necessary to authenticate and therefore believe in what we were teaching. Obviously, that is not morally or legally acceptable in our current age.

Since we cannot do this, we rely on the living tests that our spiritual ancestors were forced to conduct for us. The ancestors of our ryu had to engage their art against agressors who threatened to destroy all that was precious to their lives. We, their descendants, can learn from the validation of their experiences.

Q. *Couldn't a new art be tested out in the full-contact competitive ring under reasonably safe conditions, where the results could be discerned by all? If a technique was not effective, it wouldn't be included for long.*

A. For many reasons, the ring is no place to test out a combat-oriented self-protection art. Those "reasonably safe conditions" that would keep the event legal and moral would prevent the full utilization of the fighter's powers of intention. In the ring, after all, the fighters are not going at each other knowing that death is the certain result of losing. It should also be noted that protective gear can come to be relied upon, for both its qualities of reducing the effectiveness of otherwise damaging techniques, as well as its ability to provide a shield that can create a false image of reality in the fighter's mind. The student might end up throwing out valid techniques that would have worked without the boxing gloves, or could end up relying on techniques that would not have worked at all without the gloves. The street and field is a far different world with far different demands than are realized in the ring.

Q. *Couldn't we create a new pragmatic combat art based then on a collection of only the best technique methods from a broad range of different historical martial arts?*

A. In the first place, contrary to what may be popular belief, there are very very few combat-oriented martial arts still being taught in the world. The vast majority of martial arts seem to be presented as sports or recreation systems today. At any rate, a given collection of varying pieces of different arts all thrown together does not necessarily result in a single unified art. There needs to be some sort of recognizable key element of fundamental essence around which the art takes shape. The martial arts in general are not at all a universal body of knowledge, really, when you look carefully at the radically different approaches that characterize the movements and theories of jujutsu, all the sytles of karate, kenjutsu, aikido, not to mention the myriad systems from China. I disagree with the more popular trend towards creating "patchwork-quilt" hybrid martial arts that became a fashionable way of thinking during the 1970s.

---

*"There is no way to escape the reality of the
need to be tuned in to the greater scope
of all the elements that work together to make up
any given conflict scenario."*

Q. *With all your emphasis on combat realism, wouldn't it be a logical idea to take your system into one of the many conventional wars that are going on in the world today and try it out there?*
A. Only if you are willing to accept the fatal consequences that your universe will provide you for unnecessarily involving yourself in needless violence. There have indeed been persons who delighted in taking their theories out into random dirty little wars, street-mentality feuds, and the like, and promptly had their lives ruined as a result of their lack of foresight.

There is so much more to a true warrior art than mere mechanical technique alone. There is no way to escape the reality of the need to be tuned in to the greater scope of all the elements that work together to make up any given conflict scenario. Conventional definitions of right and wrong, strong and weak, superior and inferior, so often warp or vanish in the all-piercing light of cosmic history. Unfortunately, those realities of universal scheme and intention in the playing out of contention are most often left out due to ignorance when people set out on their own without an experienced teacher to guide them.
Q. *Is that why you place so much emphasis on the spiritual aspects of*

your warrior arts training, this area that seems to be "beyond technique"?

A. It is one of the reasons. The martial arts today seem to be mere games or toys for so many people. Students and teachers alike need to wake up to the reality of the potential danger they are playing with when it comes down to facing someone who could be determined to kill them no matter what the costs. So many teachers in so many training halls go on smugly drilling the students in techniques that haven't got a chance of working on the street against a real attacker with real intentions to humiliate or destroy. They cling aggressively to their ideas about the way "it's always been done," regardless of their lack of knowledge about historical facts or actual proven results. I have to say that is one of the greatest shames of the martial arts today.

Q. *It has been said that ninjutsu will be known as the martial art of the 1980s, just as judo was the art of the 1950s, karate the art of the 1960s, and kung-fu the art of the 1970s. But if that is to be true, how can it come about with the small number of people you have licensed as black belt teachers in the art?*

A. That reference indicates the art's impact on the martial arts community as a whole, and is not necessarily a statement regarding the numbers of people involved in the art, or the possibility of there being a ninja school in every neighborhood.

Ninjutsu is one of the few martial arts left in the world that focuses on self-protection without diluting the teachings for the sake of sport or recreation. We are already seeing a new awareness of the total warrior ideal in the martial arts press and entertainment media as a direct result of the wave of publicity given to the art of ninjutsu. Many martial artists are no longer satisfied with the crudeness of mere mechanics, the frivolity of ego-building contests, or the false glory of politically assigned belt ranks. All aspects of personal survival are under investigation now—weapons, psychology, use of nature, and anything else that will guarantee success. At last the martial arts are on their way back to having something to do with "martialness."

A second aspect, introduced by the books in the Ohara series and by the seminars we have been presenting over the past few years, is the emergence of pragmatic spiritual teaching as a necessary and working part of warrior training, not just something tacked on as an afterthought or for the sake of covering up gaps in a teacher's limited knowledge. For years, students have been hearing all the cliches about the "mental aspects" of the martial arts, but until now there has been very little attempt or ability on the part of the vast majority of instructors to present any of this kind of knowledge to their students in a useful form.

Q. *As the first non-Japanese person to ever earn full shidoshi teaching credentials from the grandmaster of ninjutsu, how do you feel about the sudden emergence of all the self-proclaimed teachers of the art that you originally introduced to the Western world?*

A. As long ago as July 1980, I was quoted in BLACK BELT magazine as saying that I was surprised that some less-than-scrupulous person "somewhere hasn't started a ninja school, teaching a little karate with some weapons to cash in on (the art). I'm really amazed that nobody has done that yet, because they do it with all the other arts." Ironically enough, at that time there were no other individuals claiming to teach ninjutsu, at least not publicly acknowledged. That unfortunately was only a temporary situation, in that the market is now flooded with all sorts of totally unqualified persons claiming that they too teach ninjutsu, now that the art has become so popular.

The thing that I cannot understand is why students are willing to believe in and pay money to a teacher who has no credentials, no evidence of any connection with a recognized master teacher of the art, and who is a living contradiction to everything that has ever been written about the authentic art and its legitimate teachers.

"Though I moved to Japan to study ninjutsu as a generic art, . . . I found that the reality was that Masaaki Hatsumi is ninjutsu in the land of the art's origin."

Q. *Couldn't the potential student ask to see the teacher's license to validate his claims?*

A. Obviously, anyone teaching ninjutsu without an authentic license from the grandmaster of the art is more than suspect of deluding the public. But these characters often tell their students that their master died the day before he was going to hand over all the scrolls, or that their old master did not believe in giving out written licenses, or they just go out and print up their own licenses themselves.

Q. *Well at least if someone is teaching Dr. Hatsumi's Bujinkan dojo ninpo system, students can tell that they are getting the real thing.*

A. Unfortunately, that is not even true any more. Since my books started to appear, several people in America and Europe have deliberately avoided the licensed teachers in the Western world and jetted to Japan for a token visit with Dr. Hatsumi or one of his instructors there in order to get some sort of low-grade ranking or a snapshot which then appears as "proof" that the impostor has indeed "studied ninjutsu in Japan with Masaaki Hatsumi." I have even heard stories that there are people using souvenir snapshots taken with me after one of my seminars in America or Europe as their "credentials" for teaching Bujinkan dojo warrior arts in their home town. No, it is still a matter of the buyer having to be extremely cautious.

Q. *You always make it sound as though your teacher's ninjutsu ryu are the only ones left in the world. Isn't it possible that some others could have survived as well?*

A. Though other writers would have readers believe that there are yet several ninjutsu ryu actively teaching in Japan, the sad truth is that almost all have vanished due to lack of interest among the post-samurai age Japanese. During my years as a permanent resident of Japan, I visited many dojo and persons said to be teaching ninjutsu, always to find disappointing results. Heishichiro Okuse, the retired mayor of Iga-Ueno City, is an aging scholar of historical ninjutsu writings and not a practitioner as was reported in a popular English language book on Japan's ninja. The Tenshin Shoden Katori Shinto ryu, which is described as teaching aspects of ninjutsu according to the authors of two completely different books, is in reality a very formal and traditional school of the samurai fighting arts. The teachers refer to instructing about ninjutsu, but the approach is geared toward how to defeat a ninja, and not how to become one. The students of the Katori Shinto school would feel offended and insulted to be referred to as studying ninjutsu. Yumio Nawa, another teacher reported to be teaching ninjutsu, is in reality an antique dealer who refers to himself as a *ninjutsu kenkuka*, (researcher of ninjutsu). Nawa does teach Japanese short chain and jo staff methods at a city recreation center every Saturday morning, but does not refer to his classical budo training group as a ninjutsu school.

I made these disappointing discoveries by living and traveling throughout Japan for the past ten years. While some American martial artists anxious to open up their own independent ninja schools will find this information to be annoying, or even angering, the undeniable facts remain openly waiting for anyone who wishes to travel to Japan and retrace the exhausting search that I have made over the years. I did not originally go to Japan for the purpose of training with Masaaki Hatsumi, though that is what I did eventually do. I went to Japan simply to study ninjutsu, and found after many dead ends that Dr. Masaaki Hatsumi was the only accredited teacher of the ninja arts recognized by the martial arts, educational, and public broadcasting circles in Japan.

Though I moved to Japan to study ninjutsu as a generic art, perhaps even under several instructors at the same time, I found that the reality was that Masaaki Hatsumi *is* ninjutsu in the land of the art's origin. I have been that man's faithful disciple ever since I came upon that discovery.

Q. *Some martial artists feel that the image of the masked ninja is a negative thing. There is something about a mask that can lead the wearer to believe that his anonymity grants him the license to get away with anything he desires, regardless of consequences or morality. What kind of effect do you think this is having on children who are fascinated with ninjutsu?*

A. It is all a question of perspective. Our school books are filled with stories of how the "mask of anonymity" provided the only possible means of accomplishment for people we are taught to regard as heroes of history. All Christians realize that the secret meetings hidden away in the catacombs of Rome were once the only means of escaping the persecution that threatened to eradicate the leaders of the fledgling religion in its early days. Colonial rebels in Boston once donned Indian disguises to allow themselves to carry out a tea-destroying protest against oppressive taxation in the days that lead to the founding of the United States of America. In numerous wartime economies around the world, anonymous underground black market activities have often provided the only sources of crucial or life-saving goods and services needed for survival by a desperate citizenry. The wartime French underground resistance movement, the escape of the Dalai Lama from Communist occupied Tibet, and the anti-slavery Underground Railway of pre-Civil War America are all additional examples of times when disappearing behind the mask of anonymity was the only means of survival. This method of perseverance and endurance for the sake of our families' survival is the only reference to masks that we ever make in our ninjutsu dojo.

Q. *Do you have any regrets about your work in the art of ninjutsu? Are there any negative aspects to your success?*

A. In the first place, I really can not consider myself a "success" in the art yet, not when I compare myself with my own teacher's abilities and skills. Regardless of any title or rank that I might have been given, I still must consider myself yet a seeker on the path.

Of course there are minor annoyances that must be put up with because of all the publicity given the art and my role in it. This is to be expected, I suppose. With the study of nin-po everything is considered to be a part of the training.

Also I have had to literally fight my way through some of my own seminars on occasion, physically downing less than mature individuals whose negative attitudes carried them away in their need to see if my art "really works." Of course my art works, but I hate to have to damage people in order to demonstrate the beauty of ninjutsu's combat effectiveness. You just cannot safely "spar" with the kind of methods we teach. Bodies get torn or broken. Realistic self-protection training is no game.

One more regrettable aspect of all the attention is the fact that I can no longer personally respond to all the mail that comes in to me from sincere people all over the world. We receive hundreds of letters every month, and have to rely on a staff of people to get information back to those who write in to us about ninjutsu. I wish that there were some way that I could more personally encourage those who have been inspired enough by this life art to write in to me. Alas, I can not find a way other than through my books and personal teaching, and so I have to consider enduring as a part of my training as well.

"The real art, the one tested and proven by history, is there for those willing to take on all that the ninja warrior lifestyle means."

Q. *In one sentence, what would you say was the purpose of ninjutsu training?*
A. The joy of freedom and lightness of the spirit, as attained through an intimate understanding of the natural universal laws of physical reality.
Q. *Is that a modern definition, or does that refer to the historical ninja as well?*
A. That is the way it always has been, and will be. The art is timeless; only the personalities that embody the art come and go with the changes of time.
Q. *What advice would you have for readers who would like to get involved in ninjutsu training?*
A. The tough truth is that there are very, very few qualified teachers of the authentic ninja arts out there, and finding a real ninjutsu teacher

worthy of your respect will not be an easy task. You can, however, take heart in the knowledge that the real art, the one tested and proven by history, is there for those willing to take on all that the ninja warrior lifestyle means. Certainly it means giving up a lot of comforts and changing your life, even moving to a new city or country perhaps, but the knowledge is there for those who really want it.

Persons interested in investigating the possibilities of getting involved with ninjutsu training can first join the Shadows of Iga Ninja Society, the international organization established in 1975 for the dissemination of information regarding training in the authentic Japanese art of ninjutsu. For information, write to the society's correspondence center at:

Shadows of Iga Ninja Society
P.O. Box 1947
Kettering, Ohio 45429-0947 USA